CHALLENGE CUP

Spectators crowded round the fourteenth tee for the closely fought semi-final of the Cornish Ladies' Golf Championship at Lelant Golf Club in 1987. The highlight of the action was a spectacular mis-hit by Sonia Harvey, which struck spectator Mrs Mary Rowe on the forearm. A search began for the ball while Mrs Rowe nursed her arm which was rapidly showing signs of bruising. The hunt drew a complete blank until Mrs Rowe's friend, Peggy White of St Ives, felt a strange discomfort in her brassiere. A discreet investigation revealed it to be the missing ball.

'Tournament Officials,' according to one report, 'declared Peggy White's bosom a natural hazard, and Miss Harvey was asked to play from the spot at which Mrs White was standing when the ball was pocketed.'

Also by Graham Nown:

CRIMINAL RECORDS

BYE BYE BIRDIE

Great Golfing Disasters

Graham Nown

Illustrated by Albert

Futura

A Futura Book
Text copyright © Graham Nown
Illustrations copyright © Alfred Rusling

First published in Great Britain in 1988 by
Futura Publications, a Division of
Macdonald & Co (Publishers) Ltd
London & Sydney

ISBN 0 7088 4048 5

Photoset in North Wales by
Derek Doyle & Associates, Mold, Clwyd.
Printed and bound in Great Britain by
Hazell, Watson & Viney Ltd
Aylesbury, Bucks

Futura Publications
A Division of
Macdonald & Co (Publishers) Ltd
Greater London House
Hampstead Road
London NW1 7QX

A member of Maxwell Pergamon Publishing Corporation plc

CONTENTS

CONTENTS

FORE! WORD

Towards the end of a court case in 1914, in which one irate golfer sued another after being hit in the eye by an errant ball, the judge was moved to give a legal definition of the Royal and Ancient game.

'Golf,' intoned Mr Justice Street, 'is a game that involves the propulsion of a small, hard ball by various types of percussion instrument, resulting in balls reaching a high rate of speed over considerable distances. In view of human frailty it is impossible to control with complete accuracy the flight of the ball, which is apt to take an erratic course.'

Judge Street neatly summed up a problem which has confronted golfers for centuries and turned a relatively simple sport into a glorious obsession. If all the energy concentrated on such a quest for perfection could somehow be harnessed, golfers might take over the world. On the other hand, it may be significant that most of the people who *do* run the world are also fanatical golfers.

The lengths to which some golfers carry their enthusiasm is quite amazing. One Canadian professional had three children: he called his son Par, and his daughter Birdie. When the third child arrived husband and wife fell out over the choice of a name. Eventually they settled on Dormie – a term used to describe a side as many holes up as there are holes left to be played.

The stories in this little volume reflect the glorious obsession people have with golf – a rugged determination to continue playing amid earthquake, fire and pestilence – and the minefield of disasters waiting on those deceptively tranquil greens.

It is a game of winners and losers, with no way of predicting what the outcome might be. The moral to all this lies in a cautionary tale of two amateurs from Montreal, Rex Matthewson and John Reagan, who each happened to fall in love with the same dazzling girl. To add to their problems, she admitted to liking them both equally. When each felt the urge to marry her they decided to settle things the civilized way, over a round of golf. In the time-honoured manner of myth and legend, whoever won the game would have the first opportunity to propose.

After a gripping, gruelling, cliffhanger of a round, Matthewson managed to beat Reagan by just one stroke, and lost no time in hurrying breathlessly off to ask for the girl's hand.

She turned him down because, as she had to admit, she could never resist a loser. *Bye Bye Birdie*, you will discover, is full of them.

Graham Nown
Birkdale

UNEXPECTED OBSTACLES

GREAT BALLS OF FIRE

The heat can play dastardly tricks with a man and, it would seem, even more so with golf balls. In Baltimore, USA, in 1959 a golfer drove off from the tee in a temperature of more than 100 degrees. Both he and his companions were shocked to see the ball begin to burn up on its seventy-five yard flight, and then disintegrate in a mid-air explosion, spreading debris over a wide area which started grass fires on the course.

There was later some uncertainty as to how this pioneer space shot was covered by the rules.

A surfeit of hi-tech theory has gone into the design of the modern golf ball. There are claims that the most aerodynamically perfect model was sketched by maths teacher Peter Reynolds on the back of a soggy beer-mat in the saloon bar of the Cransworth Arms in 1978.

Mr Reynolds, who does not even play golf, suggested a dodecahedron – the oldest design for a sphere, discovered by Plato in 400 BC. His friend Bob Haines, head of research and

'He's got it down to twenty a day'

development at Dunlop Sports, was immediately interested because the familiar dimpled version had not changed since 1934. After five years' research the DDH, as it was christened, sold feverishly in America and Japan.

A far cry from golf pro Bill Bolger of Sydney, Australia, who preferred a simpler method of producing hot-shots. Mr Bolger used to stick a golf ball in his pipe and smoke it before a big match. It was probably nothing more than a pipe-dream, but he swore that a warm ball could travel five yards further than a cold one.

BARE-FACED CHEEK

Some golfers will blame the slightest thing for putting them off their stroke. The local club at Burnham-on-Sea, Somerset, objected to plans for a nudist beach next to its links in 1984, claiming that the sight of bare bottoms would ruin players' concentration.

WHAT A YARN

Apart from the obvious need for a full survival kit, there have been suggestions that trained sniffer dogs would be useful for tracking down lost balls. At times, the odd collie might be usefully added to the list, too.

Golfers at Brighton were seen chasing a flock of sheep down the fairway in 1923 when a lost ball was spotted embedded in the thick fleece of one of them.

WHO SAID GOLF WAS RELAXING?

The problem of playing a superior opponent always presents a daunting prospect. Terrible damage can be wreaked on a golfer's confidence but, thankfully, there are a few unorthodox remedies.

Two unevenly matched players were reported to have struck a deal in 1927. With six strokes between them, the weaker player bargained for three, plus the right to shout 'Boo!' three times during the game.

At the most critical moments he would lean forward, as though preparing to give the stronger player the fright of his life, only to step back again at the last second and lapse into silence.

The tactic proved so nerve-wracking that he won the match, having given vent to only one of his three authorized 'boos'.

BAR NONE

Nigel Denham proved that no obstacle was too great to impede his progress in the 1974 English Amateur Strokeplay Championship at Moortown, near Leeds.

The disappointment he felt when his ball soared over the green deepened as he watched it strike the hard pathway leading to the clubhouse, and bounce up the steps through the open door.

Inside, he discovered that, through a series of rebounds from walls and other obstacles, it had come to rest on the carpet in front of the bar. Mr Denham, who first had to remove his spiked shoes before entering the clubhouse, sized up the situation. He opened the window, addressed the ball and dropped it neatly on the green, twenty yards away, where it came to rest just four yards from the flag.

The all-powerful Rules of Golf Committee later adjudicated that he should have forfeited two strokes because it was against the rules to open the window. The barman, at least, was immensely relieved that he had.

KEEP ON TRUCKING

At St Andrews in 1928 a ball bounced onto a nearby roadway and was promptly reduced to something resembling an omelette beneath the wheels of a passing lorry. A new ball was immediately placed on the busy spot and the player, buffeted in the slipstream of heavy traffic, nervously continued.

CHALLENGE CUP

Spectators crowded round the fourteenth tee for the closely fought semi-final of the Cornish Ladies' Golf Championship at Lelant Golf Club in 1987. The highlight of the action was a spectacular mis-hit by Sonia Harvey, which struck spectator Mrs Mary Rowe on the forearm. A search began for the ball while Mrs Rowe nursed her arm which was rapidly showing signs of bruising. The hunt drew a complete blank until Mrs Rowe's friend, Peggy White of St Ives, felt a strange discomfort in her brassiere. A discreet investigation revealed it to be the missing ball.

'Tournament officials,' according to one report, 'declared Peggy White's bosom a natural hazard, and Miss Harvey was asked to play from the spot at which Mrs White was standing when the ball was pocketed.'

The story prompted a reader to contact the *Daily Telegraph* the following week, recalling a similar incident at Hampstead Golf Club. The lady in question, from Highgate, was struggling to fight her way out of a bunker. Her ball struck the upper rim of the sand pit, and bounced back to disappear down the front of her blouse.

'To the surprise of her companion,' the *Telegraph* reported, 'she walked straight onto the green, lifted the blouse and attempted to drop the ball into the hole. She missed.'

LONG SHOT

The heyday of colonial golf, when players could pitch and putt against a backdrop of spectacular scenery and tropical sunsets, is largely gone. Civilization may have seemed a pleasantly hazy prospect, but natural hazards loomed larger than on the pastel hills of Blighty.

A golfer at Barrackpore, near Calcutta, for instance, watched as his ball was picked up by a large back carrion crow in 1899. The bird flew off and dropped it conveniently just inches from the pin. As he prepared to sink his unexpected windfall, the player gleefully remarked to his companion, 'I bet this hole has never been done in two.'

It still hasn't. At that moment there was a severe earthquake, and the result was a hole-in-one. Any satisfaction was tempered by the fact that the hole was so enormous that the golfer was lucky not to disappear along with his ball.

A CANNY SCOT

At the turn of the century, Scottish amateur Freddie Tait searched for his ball in the rough and found it lodged neatly in the bottom of a discarded can of condensed milk.

The seemingly insurmountable problem was solved when he pitched the can – and its contents – in a high arc onto the green. The can landed, tipping out the ball within perfect striking distance of the hole.

THE ROCKET-POWERED BALL

In the Spring of 1985, greenkeeper Peter Jordan sat patiently on his tractor waiting for a group of players to finish on the fourteenth green in the distance.

When the last of the group had teed-off, about 130 yards away, Mr Jordan turned the ignition key to continue with his grass cutting. Nothing happened. When he tried again, the engine coughed and wheezed and died a second time. Suspecting that his tractor was being temperamental, the determined greenkeeper kept on trying to fire the engine.

At about the twentieth attempt, success came with a tremendous build-up of engine gases and a small explosion which culminated in a round white missile being fired like a cannonball from the vertical exhaust of the tractor.

The golf ball flew hundreds of feet into the air, arched in a slow trajectory, and then crashed onto the roof of a house almost fifty yards away. The impact drew the attention of the golfers who watched it rebound, soar over two bunkers, bounce onto the green and roll sweetly to within a club-length of the hole.

The golfer who had made the original drive walked over, assessed the situation, and putted for a birdie two.

Mr Jordan, who tended the greens at Combe Wood, Kingstone, Surrey, had not heard the ball rattle into his exhaust pipe because of the noise of another tractor which was passing at the time.

'The man who hit the ball gave me a big thumbs-up and called, "Thank you very much",' he said.

BOAT STATIONS

One of golf's oddest interruptions occurred at St Andrews in 1860 as players were driving off for their Autumn Meeting.

It was a wild, squally day on which only the most hardy ventured out. Midway through the game news arrived that a ship had gone down off the Eden. When a distress call went out, the golfers, to a man, launched a convenient rowing boat into the surf and set off to the rescue.

They battled out against rough, fast-running seas and managed to save the ship's crew from certain disaster. After depositing them safely they rowed feverishly back, scrambled up the beach soaking wet and immediately resumed the abandoned game.

RETURN TICKET

If comedian George Burns had no affection for string instruments before a tournament between Pennsylvania State University and the University of Maryland, he most certainly had later. A wild Burns slice cleared an adjoining railway line and seemed destined for oblivion in a factory yard, when fortune intervened.

The ball, travelling at tremendous speed, hit some overhead telephone wires, bent them taut like a catapult and shot back with renewed propulsion onto the green. Burns chomped on his cigar with satisfaction as the ball came to rest just two club-lengths from the hole.

AN ELECTRIFYING PERFORMANCE

There are times when every golfer would welcome a helping hand from heaven and, on occasions, it has been known to happen with unexpected results. Struggling young golf pro John Brennard was trying desperately for a place in an under-25's tournament at Sunningdale, when the sky suddenly darkened.

Fearing rain, he put up his umbrella and walked to his ball, 55 feet from the pin. Without warning, the tip of the brolly was struck by a freak bolt of lightning which sent a tremendous shock down his left shoulder and leg.

Incredibly, Mr Brennard emerged unsinged. But instead of finding himself in a state of nervous devastation, he felt strangely galvanized into pushing on to victory.

'I found myself playing like a champ,' he admitted after winning the trophy. 'Being struck by lightning opened up a whole new world for me. Before Sunningdale things had been a bit lean.'

TALE OF A TREE IRON

Michael Donaldson was undaunted when his second shot of the day at Scotland's Carricknowe golf course soared into a tree and lodged firmly in the branches. Bernhard Langer's

famous tree shot of 1982 provided Mr Donaldson with confidence and inspiration.

He clambered up, Tarzan-style, ignoring his
friend Alistair Graham's claim that he would
have to drop a stroke. As Mr Donaldson steadied
himself to address the ball, Mr Graham played
his second stroke. There was a brief cry of 'Fore'
before his ball took off and landed inches from
the same spot, breaking Mr Donaldson's ankle.

The game had to be abandoned while Mr
Donaldson was brought down from the tree and
taken to hospital for treatment.

This leafy legend was eclipsed only by the
story of a lady golfer in Sydney, Australia,
whose first drive landed in the fork of a tree. She
declared it unplayable and drove off again. The
second ball landed in the same tree, where it
knocked the first ball back onto the course
before wedging itself immovably in the
branches.

BALLS, LOST AND WISELY
ABANDONED

NOW YOU SEE IT …

Missing golf balls support a whole manufacturing industry. Those eventually found turn up in the unlikeliest places – as the player who sliced into a pond from a fairway near Glasgow will testify.

He waded in to retrieve it and, in accordance with the rules, found a patch of dry ground and dropped it over his shoulder. Despite being carefully watched by two partners keen to spot infringements, no one could find the ball.

A thorough search was made of the surrounding area until it was finally discovered – in the hood of his anorak.

KEEPING AHEAD OF THE PLAY

Golfers have been known to favour eccentric hats, but none could compete with the headgear chosen by pensioner Robert Lees, who lived alongside the fourth green of Elderslie Golf Club, Scotland.

On fine days he could be seen pottering in his garden wearing a dustbin lid, tied coolie-fashion beneath his chin by a securing strap. For sixteen years, mowing the lawn was a survival course, dodging stray balls which soared over his hedge.

The artillery began almost as soon as the fourth green was completed in 1967. Mr Lees received a whack on the head, and a friend was laid flat on the lawn by another stray ball. He ceased to count the near misses.

Mr Lees repaired broken garage windows and straightened demolished flower beds, while his family refused point blank to set foot in the garden. He covered his windows in wire mesh, built a six-foot-high fence, and encouraged his hedge to grow to twelve feet – and still the balls kept winging over.

Mr Lees collected more than 200 as souvenirs and gave away the rest to local children. In excess of 500, he estimated, whistled off course into his garden – a withering testimony to the standard of play at Elderslie. All the golfers involved were too embarrassed to ask for their balls back.

Mr Lees finally hung up his dustbin bonnet in 1983 when the club applied for planning permission to erect a high fence between his garden and the fourth green.

CAUGHT OUT

Just how far will a golfer go in search of a lost ball, rather than incur a penalty stroke? A player at Royal Lytham in the early 1920s sliced badly down by the railway. His ball rose gracefully over the fence, just as a slow goods train was passing.

The engine driver saw it coming, stretched out his hand and, incredibly, managed to catch it. Despite the pleas of the golfer panting alongside the clanking train, still clutching his club, the driver refused to hand it over, saying he would treasure it all his life.

FEELING UNDER PAR

Napper the labrador found it hard to subdue his retrieving instincts. His favourite tee-time treat during walkies on the golf course near his home at Stoneydelph, near Tamworth, Staffordshire, was any golf ball he came across.

Napper's taste for them waned slightly after swallowing fifteen on a single afternoon jaunt. His owner, Elizabeth Hall, found two in the garden, then Napper regurgitated another six. It took the local vet to remove the remaining seven under anaesthetic.

SCALES OF JUSTICE

In 1933, golfer John Cathcart met with a new handicap on the course near his home in Florida when a ten-foot alligator snapped up his ball and waddled off with it. Mr Cathcart decided not to press for ownership.

THE BOOMER-RANG

Crowds at the *Daily Mail* golf tournament at St Anne's in 1923 might have been forgiven for thinking that French champion Aubrey Boomer was something of a magician. At the eighth hole he played his shot, but the ball hit a bank, rocketed into the air and vanished from sight.

Boomer himself was rather mystified. He searched, along with his caddie and officials, without success. Then he found the ball – it had landed in the right-hand pocket of his golfing jacket.

JAIL BIRDIES

There are severe penalties governing the search for lost balls at Northeye eighteen-hole course near Bexhill, Essex. Among the more daunting is the prospect of a stiff jail sentence.

As clubs go, Northeye is quite exclusive. It was built for the inmates of H.M. Prison, and a player's excuse that he was shinning the twelve-foot-high fence, topped with barbed wire, to search for a ball is greeted with a distinct lack of sympathy.

The 1,767-yard, par 30 course, equipped with a dozen sets of clubs provided by the Home Office, is the only prison course in Britain. A quarter of the jail's 430 residents have played – without a single absentee by the time they get to the eighteenth.

NOT TO BE SNIFFED AT

Lost balls are a perennial problem, but a Californian chemist came up with a solution. He sold balls impregnated with perfume in the theory that they would attract butterflies when lost in the rough. He was last heard of working on the problem of how to find balls before butterflies hatch. Trained caterpillars were not considered a marketable proposition.

A SLICE OF LIFE

Emilio and Margaret Punzo had to pay an extra £5,000 for their dream home because of its prime position overlooking the ninth tee of San Ramon golf course near San Francisco. It took only a few weeks to discover that the wild slices of local golfers turned domestic bliss into a nightmare.

Five years later, after countless broken roof tiles, smashed windows and battered walls, the house conjured up scenes from the last days of the Alamo. The Punzos took 2,000 golf balls to court to prove their point and were awarded a cash settlement, plus a new house guaranteed to be miles from the nearest golf course.

Friends around the corner, whose home faced the thirteenth fairway, collected 8,000 golf balls. They were last heard of considering similar action.

WATCH THE BIRDIE

All creatures great and small, it would seem, are extremely partial to the little white ball. Two women players on the Ballycastle links, in County Antrim, were astonished to see a seagull swoop down at a crucial point in the game and fly away with the ball, which was never seen again.

This was perhaps bettered only by a gull at the

seaside course of Dunskey, Wigtownshire, where a woman drove into the rough and the bird obligingly picked up the ball and dropped it back on the fairway.

Delighted, and swift to seize the advantage, she squared-up for a chip-shot to the green. At that very moment the gull swooped back, snatched up the ball and carried it out to sea.

In the 1920s, during a match between Raynes Park and Surbiton, a flight of crows descended and, in the general confusion, absconded with four balls.

They were perhaps related to the crow which flew off with 450 balls in six months at South Herts Golf Club in 1962. Its score was marginally above that of the squirrel which stored 120 balls in a hollow tree at Montreal golf course in 1930. The collection was estimated to have taken almost seven years' hard work to put together – dedication worthy of many a golfer.

At Hoylake, where a selective family of crows would fly away with only new balls, the Royal Liverpool secretary told members that the committee had no objection to their carrying shotguns in their golf bags.

Birds, however, have a strong sense of natural justice. Two players in a singles competition at Fulwell Golf Club, Hampton Hill, had just played their approach shots to one of the greens when a pair of rooks swooped, simultaneously seized a ball each and took off with them into the trees.

Some balls, on the other hand, are perhaps best left unretrieved. In 1903, a player in Cairo was searching vainly for his lost ball when a snake darted from the rough, grabbed it in its jaws, and disappeared down a hole.

A club official, seasoned by such mishap, remarked that the snake had probably mistaken it for an egg. Hard-boiled, presumably.

HARD TO SWALLOW

A Madras newspaper carried a report in 1920 of a hawk which had swooped on a local golf course and carried away a ball. Some weeks later the bird was found dead alongside the missing ball. A post-mortem, carried out by a local vet, revealed that the hawk had died from acute anxiety brought on by trying unsuccessfully to hatch it out.

HORNSWOGGLED

Fifteen balls were gobbled up by a hungry herd of Aberdeen Angus cows in the course of a tournament at Gainsborough, Lincolnshire, in 1955.

ON THE BALL

Bournemouth Council were asked in 1972 to resurrect a nineteenth-century bye-law which declared that no-one other than a golfer could search for lost balls.

A spokesman for the director of parks said, 'We found that certain people have trained their dogs specially to sniff out and look for golf balls, and are making a living selling them back to golfers.'

SQUARE PEGS AND ROUND HOLES

SINKING THEM NICELY

In the early 1930s an unnamed English scratch golfer was reported to have agreed to give his very average opponent a sporting chance by drinking a glass of scotch on each green during an eighteen-hole match.

The old hand won the first six holes effortlessly. Then his driving became noticeably erratic, and a slight weave was detected in his walk. By the twelfth, the influence had become more marked and he was only two up.

Contemporary accounts claim that he won the thirteenth only by spontaneously bursting into song as his partner took a vital putt. Amazingly, he still had a lead of one when he reached the seventeenth tee, despite giving the appearance of walking uphill.

Here, alas, he came to grief – the scratch player not only missed the ball completely, but fell over backwards on top of it. Finally, with ignominy, he was forced to concede defeat when – as they say in boxing – he found himself unable to rise.

GOLF CHUMPIONS

In the best traditions of fearless journalism, *Golf Digest* dredged the courses of America for the outstanding duffers of golf. A daunting and dangerous mission – out there dodging balls and flying divots, hysterical hooks and wild slices. Never has the courage of the golfing reporter been more keenly tested.

As one newspaper put it, 'these are the shimmeringly dismal people who hit tee shots into their own golf bags, and don't use a golf cart because they need to go where golf carts cannot, who hook into hotel rooms and passing trucks, who get refunds from teaching professionals after one lesson.'

Golfers who qualified needed to be outstandingly bad. A minimum twenty-one rounds a year were required to enter. Hundreds of hopefuls – yes, some people will do anything for a title – were whittled down to a dozen. Then, after eliminating heats, the big play-off came in 1985. Spectators were expected to bring their own hard-hats.

Giants included Ray Walker, who dropped 327 consecutive balls into a pond at a course in Florida, and Chief Warrant Officer Richard Gonzales, who made a remarkable advance of four yards after eleven dynamic strokes.

Then there was Neil Hamlin who carded fifty-five on one hole, and the memorable winner, Angelo Spagnolo, who lost thirteen balls in the process of scoring 161. The record for the shortest drive, which still stands – and, indeed, probably always will – was minus nine yards.

Is the future of terrible golf safe? *Golf Digest* confidently forecasts that there is worse to come: 'The reservoir of truly horrific golfing talent in this great land of ours is deeper and more plentiful than we dared hope for,' the magazine reports.

MOONSTRUCK

One evening in 1890, Lord Kennedy, leaning on the bar at the Montrose Golf Club, challenged a Mr Cruickshank to three holes of golf at £500 a hole. The only proviso was that they played then and there.

It was 10.30 pm, and the course lay in pitch darkness under a bomber's moon. No lights were available, except for a lantern which someone luckily produced to wave near the hole.

A crowd turned out to watch – or attempt to watch – the curious game. Local boys were summoned from bed and stationed round the course. They were ordered to strain their ears for the whistle of golf balls and run to the spot where they landed. Records of who won no longer exist, but curiously, both players were so familiar with the course that they went round in almost the same number of strokes they normally played in daylight.

One of the game's more eccentric players, John Ball, had an unusual round at Hoylake in 1907.

He took to the links in dense fog, aided only by a ball hastily painted black, and completed the course in eighty – one less than many of his friends could manage in good visibility.

An important match staged by Essex Professional Golfers' Union in 1926 attracted an
enormous number of entries.

So many, in fact, that worried organizers
noticed the light failing long before players had
reached the home green. By the seventeenth,
players were having difficulty seeing each other
in the gloom.

At the eighteenth, the sun had set and it was
impossible to see the hole. The tournament was
completed only by the help of dedicated club
members lying on the green holding lighted
matches.

Forty golfers at Scotscraig Golf Club, Fife, played
an odd game in total darkness with the aid of
flashlights in 1983. In the course of play, which
lasted from dusk until dawn hundreds, perhaps
even thousands, of luminous balls were lost.

They had considerably better luck than two
players who attempted a round at Old Trafford
in 1910. It was a moonless night, perfect for
poachers moving around the nearby woods, but
hopeless for golf. Eventually the club's entire
stock of balls was exhausted – along with the
players – and the game had to be abandoned.

Moonlighting has been inexplicably popular.
Mr E.F. Storey, secretary of Cambridge University Golf Club, finished a record round of
sixty-six in 1923 at Royal Wimbledon, with the

help of candles tied to the flags. Fortunately for Mr Storey it was a calm, windless evening.

Back in 1876 David Straith won a wager by going round St Andrew's by moonlight in less than 100 strokes.

THE ROCKY ROAD TO THE TOP

Manchester golf pro Denis Durnian had an unusual method of psyching himself up for major tournaments. He always watched Sylvester Stallone in *Rocky* before doing battle with the heavyweights of the golfing world.

'Watching Stallone gets me in the right frame of mind,' he said. 'Those films capture the feeling of someone taking on the world and winning, of a guy pulling off the impossible dream.'

Maybe there's something in it – Durnian tried it before the Royal Birkdale Open in 1983 and set a record by covering the first nine holes in twenty-eight.

'I'm convinced it was not a coincidence,' he mumbled.

PASS THE No. 5 TIN OPENER

Harry Dearth, a popular but slightly eccentric Edwardian baritone, clanked onto the links at Bushey dressed in a heavy suit of armour he had worn the previous night while playing St George in Elgar's *Masque* at the London Coliseum.

Onlookers reported that he was a 'wonderful sight', glowing with a golden hue in the May sunlight of 1912. Inside, it was a different story. Sweating profusely, risking hernia and barely able to lift his club because of the weight he was carrying, Dearth was narrowly beaten by two and one.

ONE OF THE BOYS

To ensure that young rising star Lora Fairclough had an adequate supply of suitable competition, Chorley Golf Club in Lancashire decided officially to change her sex to male.

Lora, a fourteen-year-old schoolgirl, brought down her handicap from thirty-five to one in just three years. The club changed the rules to enable her to play off men's tees and a men's handicap.

'Being a man should be good for my game,' Laura was quoted as saying.

UPS AND DOWNS

Gimmick golf matches have been many and varied, occasionally verging on the tedious: golfers vs archers, golfers pitted against light aircraft dropping flour bombs, fly fishing casting champions and amateur javelin throwers.

All this lunacy must have started somewhere, and the culprits, as far as anyone can be sure, were a Mr Smellie, an Edinburgh printer, and his companion Mr Sceales of Leith.

Between them, for a wager in 1798, they drove over the weathercock of St Giles Cathedral, a height of more than 160 ft.

From then on, golf was full of ups and downs. Tom Morris, the second Open champion, drove balls 400 ft up onto the road bridge at Ballochmyle, to keep his hand in. How passing motorists coped is not recorded.

In 1896 Freddie Tait, a subaltern in the Black Watch (and, as you may recall, the man who battled with the condensed milk tin), fulfilled a strange ambition by driving balls down from the Rockery of Edinburgh Castle.

His green was Princes Street Gardens – a mere speck 300 yards away and 350 ft below. Local residents gave him a wide berth but, incredibly, every shot was on target. However, by the time Tait had scaled down the face to take stock of his handiwork, someone had stolen his balls.

The pioneering work of Smellie and Sceales was not all in vain. In World War Two an officer was quietly practising with his niblick on the deck of the aircraft carrier *Illustrious*, when an

enemy aircraft appeared without warning and dropped a string of incendiary bombs on the ship's flight deck. The officer deftly pitched them one by one into the sea with his club.

Marathon matches take their toll, if not in physical injury, then at least in the club bar afterwards.

Two golfers played a round over a twenty-mile route in South Wales. They took 608 strokes – and finished in a state of complete exhaustion.

And in 1939 an American, J. Smith Ferebee, played from dawn until dusk on his local Chicago course, completing eight rounds – 144 holes – non-stop.

His efforts won him a plantation in Virginia and a £500 side-bet, which was a slight compensation as they carried him home suffering from blisters and lumbago.

A match of slightly longer duration dragged on for sixteen years and, even then, only finished when one of the players died.

Two pensioners from Chilton Foliat, Swindon, began hacking it out in 1922 at Littlecote links.

George New, the postmaster, died at sixty-six years, ahead by 2,437 strokes and 479 holes. He had played 86,379 strokes against the 88,816 of his seventy-five-year-old opponent, retired farmer W.R. Chamberlain.

GOLFING EVERGREENS

Mr George Jones, of Mosborough, near Sheffield, wanted to take his lifelong passion for golf beyond the grave. When he died in 1984, at the age of seventy-three, he requested in his will that his ashes be scattered on the eighteenth green of Renishaw Golf Club.

His wish was echoed by Thomas Caradonio, an avid golfer, who was buried the same year in Houston, Texas, wearing golf clothes and clutching a putter. Mr Caradonio died of a stroke – the cardiac variety – on the eighth green, and feared that his friends would fail to recognize him in a business suit.

DRIVEN TO DISTRACTION

Golf, as we all know, is a game of concentration and relaxation, but the two do not necessarily go hand in hand. Americans are so influenced by watching the great men of the game on television that they try to ape them at every opportunity.

Every weekend-golfer behaves as though he is competing in the United States Open – pacing out shots, and sighting angles along the line of his club. Actor Sean Connery became so irritated by these golf course theatricals that he actually gave up his favourite sport on visits to the

'You should have taken a Jeroboam from the tee'

United States. Playing a round took so long that he decided to improve his tennis instead.

BOTTLING IT UP

In the 1930s the highpoint of golfing confidence was scaled when an American player, John Montague, took on several golfers with a shovel, a rake and a baseball bat. Strangely enough he won.

His fondness for curious clubs was matched by a member of Royal St George's Sandwich, who played with a champagne bottle (empty) while his opponent used clubs.

The man with the bottle just managed to scrape home – unlike some golfers partial to a bottle who invariably crawl home.

SUPPORTING A LOST CAUSE

Dennis MacKey spent some of his happiest hours on the old Whaley Bridge course in Derbyshire. When the club folded in 1959 and was sold as farmland, the greens and holes quickly became overgrown and trampled by grazing sheep and cows.

Mr MacKey, the former captain, went back at the age of seventy-five and found that he could still pick out the raised tees and bunkers created in 1906. Old memories came flooding back. After a word with the farmer he was given permission to play the course every day, content in the knowledge that the only rabbits he would have to contend with were the bob-tailed variety.

SLOW COACHES

Do you think your game would improve if you really eased back and took it slow?

Former Open champion Bobby Locke tested the theory and played a 'slow motion' round with Henry Cotton and Reg Whitcombe – he lost six pounds with the tension.

Locke, who described it as 'the biggest ordeal I ever went through' drained himself with the intense concentration involved and sweated every putt.

CURIOUS CADDIES

THE SOLE OF DISCRETION

A certain Major J. Willoughby encountered a trainee caddy while golfing in Nigeria in 1949.

Several times, after driving into the rough, the major became quite puzzled. By the time he reached the caddy the ball was always just on the edge of the fairway.

It happened time after time until the baffled Willoughby discovered that the caddy, in an effort to create a good impression, was picking up the ball between his big toe and the next, and 'walking' it onto the fairway.

THE GOLF-WIDOW'S REVENGE

A strictly non-caddy story: somewhere out there, a silent army of long-suffering golf widows salutes the anonymous Brighton house-wife who got her revenge. Unable to bear her husband's absence any longer, she picked up his clubs one evening in 1985, walked out of the house and gave them to the first man she met.

As the astonished stranger walked home clutching his prize he was unfortunately stopped by the police, who found his explanation suspicious to say the least. The passer-by discovered that, as one door opens, another closes – he was arrested for carrying stolen property.

The golfing husband, a pub landlord, recovered his clubs when police issued a description of his tees, which were fashioned from plastic in the shape of naked women.

A spokesman for Brighton police said at the time, 'They patched up their row, but the husband begged us not to give his name – he was so embarrassed.'

JUMBO CADDY

A British civil servant in colonial India in the 1920s became so impatient at having to stoop to change clubs in the heat that he bought an elephant and trained it to caddy.

The beast, with a golf bag slung over its shoulder, was such a towering success that the golfer never employed a human caddy again. Just, presumably, someone to follow them both across the green with a shovel and bucket.

GOLFING ANGEL

To provide a moment's relief from these golfing tales of woe, one of the most glowing testimonies to the beneficial effects of the game came from former *Charlie's Angel* actress, Cheryl Ladd.

Fearful that, in the fickle world of Hollywood, she might become 'yesterday's blonde', Cheryl took up golf. She found it gave her discipline and concentration, and soon became a fanatical player. Shortly afterwards her first major film opened to critical acclaim, and Cheryl put her success down entirely to her favourite sport. She is reported to have no shortage of caddies.

FORE

'A negro caddie was struck on the forehead with so much force by the ball that it rebounded for seventy-five yards. He was unhurt save for a bit of a bump.'

Daily Dispatch, 1923

ODD BALLS

DAZZLING DRIVES

Considering the ponderous weight and eccentric balance of ancient clubs, some of those early record drives rate as Olympian achievements.

E.E. Bliss covered 445 yards at Herne Bay in August 1913. And back in 1892, Mr E. Blackwell, of St Andrew's, drove 366 yards from the last tee to the steps of the Royal and Ancient clubhouse. He also used a guttie ball which did not have the flight or carrying power of modern balls.

So far, though, no one has managed to beat the Scottish golfer whose remarkable drive from the first tee at Prestwich landed on the tender of the passing Glasgow express, which stopped thirty-eight miles away.

DIVINE INTERVENTION

The entire course of golf matches has occasionally been changed by the oddest intrusions. In 1967 a sonic boom made a ball quiver on the edge of the eighteenth hole at a London surburban course – then fall in.

Two golfers at Kirkfield, Ontario, were even as

they approached the eighteenth. The match finally depended on a long putt which stopped agonizingly on the very lip of the hole. Then, amazingly, a grasshopper alighted on the ball and it toppled in.

A STROKE OF LUCK

Every golfer's dream of a hole-in-one is almost mundane for Californian Scott Palmer. In 1984, by the age of twenty-six, he had achieved it eighteen times in one year – and hit the pin with drives on fifty other occasions.

And if that is not irritating enough, he has sworn affidavits to prove it. Palmer, clearly not of this planet, hit all but one of his aces with a seemingly indestructible ball. So far he has been offered more than £7,000 for the Spalding Top

Flite XL No. 2, and the bids are still rolling in.

The chances of the rest of us holing-in-one are calculated at 33,616 to 1. Palmer, an author, has the advantage of playing every day on the municipal Balboa Park course in San Diego.

Comedian Bob Hope had to wait thirty years for his moment of glory. When it finally came the excitement was too much. Hope fainted and had to be given brandy to revive him.

Ron Keeler, of Great Yarmouth, has holed-in-one only once. But his achievement, at Gorleston Golf Club, was hailed as truly remarkable – Mr Keeler lost his right arm in an accident some years previously.

DELAYED DROP

Golfer John Shoesmith got to the lip of the twelfth hole in two – and there the ball stayed, balanced precariously.

As the crowd watching the Star Tournament at the Royal Mid-Surrey course, Richmond, drew nearer a partridge was seen scurrying up and down, looking for a suitable way of escape.

The ball, disturbed by wind currents from the bird's wings, trickled into the hole for an albatross two – three under par – a full two minutes after the shot.

JOIN THE GOLF SET

A member, who prefers to remain anonymous, slipped out his bottom set of false teeth and put them in his jacket pocket before embarking on a round at Addlington Court, Croydon. When he returned to the clubhouse he found that his jacket and his teeth were missing.

After due consideration, Croydon Dental Services Committee rejected his application for a replacement set of dentures with the ruling: 'There would not appear to be any reason why dentures should be removed while playing golf.'

Among the flotsam and jetsam left on one golf course was a complete set of false teeth, carefully removed and placed on the green while the owner applied all his concentration to a putt. He then walked off and forgot all about them.

SURPRISE, SURPRISE

If golfers were not incorrigible optimists the game might have faded into oblivion long ago. Even when the most daunting challenge looms, hope springs eternal beneath the thickest woollen pullover.

In 1984 Peter Rawlinson half-heartedly agreed to take part in a golf competition at Thetford, in Norfolk. He had played less than a dozen rounds in his life, and it was at least two years since he had picked up the set of old clubs he had bought in a junk shop.

At the tee of the par three eighth, he selected his battered driver and gazed down the sloping 200-yard fairway before addressing the ball. Mr Rawlinson gave a hefty swing and watched the ball bounce once on the fairway before trickling across the green and disappearing into the hole.

His prize for the greatest shot of his life was a £14,500 Volvo turbo. The bill for drinks in the clubhouse later came to £178.

SLICED

A difficult-to-believe tale from the Thirties, but one supported by eye-witnesses: A greensman at Huddersfield was holding a scythe when a ball struck the blade and was cut clean in two.

PLAYING FOR TIME

Australian golfer F.D. Walter was driving off at Geelong when the strap of his watch broke. The timepiece slid from his wrist and fell onto the ball at the moment of impact.

Walter drove his watch forty yards down the fairway where he recovered it, still ticking. They don't make them like that anymore.

POCKET GOLF

Oliver P. Horlick was 100 yards from the sixteenth green at Burnham Beeches in 1923, when he felt something rattle the matchbox in his jacket pocket.

He gingerly put in his hand and felt a golf ball. It had been sliced there by a Mr Levi who apologized – then offered to play it from where it lay.

A ball driven by the professional at Sundrige Park Golf Club bounced and lodged with perfect balance on the half-inch-wide top of a boundary fence. It was played off and holed in seven.

Maintenance men repairing street lights in Stourbridge found a golf ball inside the lamp glass, 200 yards from the seventeenth tee. Even the most determined golfer would clearly be defeated by that one.

TIME FOR A DOUBLE

It took Joe McCaffrey twenty-five years to hole-in-one. And when he finally scored his ace, at the 172-yard twelfth at Vale of Leven, Dumbartonshire, there were drinks all round at the clubhouse.

His son Gordon dropped in to congratulate him before joining his partner at the first and teeing off. The game was unmemorable until he came to the twelfth and holed-in-one.

'When it landed on the green', his partner said, 'it seemed to take an eternity to reach the hole. We just stood there speechless and frozen until it dropped.'

SCORECARD SHOCKERS

In 1935 an American woman took 166 strokes to get her ball into the hole.

Her troubles began when she hit it into a river where it was swept downstream. Instead of giving up like anyone else, she stubbornly vowed to see it through.

A mile-and-a-quarter downstream she finally cornered her ball and drove off from a standing position in a rowing boat. From there with the current against her it was a long drive back.

One of the fastest rounds on record was accomplished at Cape Town in 1931 by Len Richardson, an Olympic runner who played a 6,000 yard in thirty-two – minutes that is. Presumably, his golf was on a par with his sprinting.

ON THE REBOUND

At a Sunningdale inter-club tournament in 1930 the Army and Navy ball came to grief in a bunker. Then J.E. Mellor, playing for the Royal Thames Yacht Club, managed to send his tee shot into the same bunker. To the disbelief of the services team, his ball landed squarely on the first, bounced off and rebounded onto the green, giving Mellor a three.

TRENCH WARFARE

Deep in their respective bunkers, in May 1926, both Lt. Colonel Buchanan Dunlop and Colonel Howard were convinced it was their shot. The pair, in a foursome for the Army Golfing Society against St Andrew's, played at exactly the same time.

The balls collided in mid-air and dropped on each side of the sixteenth hole, five yards apart.

MID-AIR MIRACLE

In 1928 a Dr Alcorn and a Mr Avery set off to play the Wentworth Falls course in Australia.

They were joined by Mr E. Barnes, the Leura Club professional, and at the ninth hole Barnes and Avery found themselves on opposite sides of the green.

Each played a chip shot at exactly the same moment. Dr Alcorn watched the two balls rise from different angles, touch in mid-air and both drop into the hole – a feat which has probably never since been equalled.

NOT A BAD SHOT, LOOKING BACK

Lucky the golfer who has holed in one ... but someone has yet to match the achievement of R.R. Smiley, of Goldsborough, North Carolina, who managed it backwards.

While driving off from the thirteenth hole he sliced the ball, and it came to rest squarely in the eleventh.

THE CALL OF THE WILD

WHAT A BLOW

Some players are extremely sensitive to being put off their stroke. The smallest thing can break their concentration – and indeed the largest.

Spectators at the New Zealand National Open at Ngamoutu links were unexpectedly forced to run for cover at a vital moment in the 1940s event.

A whale suddenly appeared alongside the fourteenth hole, which was right on the edge of the shore. It spouted a column of water at the astonished players and, with the help of a good tail wind, soaked them to the skin.

B-OFF

Jack Nicklaus and Gary Player failed to complete one hole during an exhibition game at Swertkop, South Africa, after being pursued by a swarm of angry killer bees. The old pros retreated, flailing the air with towels, and resumed their game elsewhere on the course.

ALL CREATURES GREAT AND SMALL

Countless stories of birds and beasts despatched by flying golf balls crop up with such regularity that the pastoral calm of the fairway begins to sound like a busy day at a Kosher abattoir.

A cow was once killed at St. Margaret's Bay golf club, Dover, but the club issued a statement that they were fortunately covered by third pary insurance.

Elsewhere a fox was hit on the head and killed; hares and weasels have met untimely deaths colliding with golf balls, and one player at Chester bagged two water wagtails with a single shot.

Another golfer once killed a partridge and raised the awkward question in the clubhouse of whether or not he had a game licence.

In the 1920s, *Golf Illustrated* reported the case of a player who sent a ball skimming low over a river to hit a 2lb salmon in mid-leap.

The force of the blow threw the fish onto the bank where it was found with the ball wedged firmly between its teeth. But that sounds more like a fisherman's tale than a golfer's.

King George V was distressed to hit a cow while golfing at Balmoral. The animal shook her head, possibly in disbelief, and to the astonishment of the Royal entourage the ball dropped out of her left ear.

Mr W.L. Wass was driving a long, low shot from the tenth tee at Thorpe Hill, Essex, when his ball hit a titlark as it rose, fifty yards away.

Ten minutes later his partner, a Mr. A.F. Hart, played a mash shot down the twelfth fairway and killed another lark in flight.

The birds were stuffed and mounted on the wall of the club lounge alongside a partridge and a greenfinch which had shared a similar fate.

GRIN AND BEAR IT

Nature, however, has fought back with tooth and claw on more than one occasion.

Earl Haig, Lady Haig and Colonel F.F. Clarke embarked on a round to celebrate the opening of a new course in the national park near Jasper, Alberta, in 1926.

As the colonel's ball came to rest, two bears trundled from a nearby forest and took turns to chew it calmly to shreds. The rule book, even in Alberta, allowed for no such contingency.

In the early 1960s a bear rampaged around Ocean Shores golf course, at Aberdeen, near Washington D.C. The club tried everything to drive it away, and eventually succeeded only with the aid of a helicopter.

Club rules were amended as follows: 'If a ball is picked up by a bear, the player may replace it and take one penalty stroke. If the player gets

the ball back from the bear, take automatic par
for hole.'

HOW SAM SNEAD WAS GIVEN THE BILL

The celebrated Sam Snead was not entirely
surprised when he saw an ostrich wander across
the rough during a South American tour. He did
become alarmed, however, when it cocked a
beady eye at his straw hat and galloped towards
his bunker.

Sam raised his arm defensively, and the
ostrich settled for second-best. The bird sank its
beak into his hand and hung on. Sam was out of
action for two weeks after the incident.

MONKEY BUSINESS

The element of surprise should never be
overlooked in the course of play in far-flung
parts. Mrs Molly Whitaker is a case in point.
When she squared up to extricate herself from a
bunker at Beachwood, South Africa, a monkey –
thought to be male – leapt on her back and
wrapped its arms round her neck.

The love-sick creature had to be beaten off by

Mrs Whitaker's caddie before play could resume.

W. Loveridge, a golf professional from Shipley, had an unnerving encounter with an extremely large toad at Redcar in 1925.

His ball, driven from the eleventh tee, landed in long grass and lodged on the back of a large toad.

As Mr Loveridge approached, the toad suddenly jumped and the ball rolled off, plopping into the hollow where it had been sitting.

When he pushed the toad out of the way, it jumped back onto the ball, and flattened it so deeply into the ground that it was rendered unplayable.

Mr Loveridge's opponent tried to invoke a penalty stroke for lifting. But as the ball had been moved by an outside agency, it could not be enforced.

Clearly golfers must be prepared for anything, as the Duke of York discovered to his cost on the Rhondda Course at Ton-Pentre in 1924.

The Duke had just played a magnificent putt, when a dog ran on, picked up the ball and dropped it on the other side of the green.

'Arrest that dog!' the Duke snorted, and lost the hole.

Golf in colonial outposts was fraught with difficulty. A player on the Chembur links in Bombay in 1946 saw his ball swallowed by a snake.

The game, as we have seen, was seldom without incident in Alberta. During one tournament, seventy-five wild elk stampeded across the thirteenth green, forcing players to abandon their clubs and scale trees for safety.

A man-eating tiger livened up play at a Hong Kong club between the wars, killing two policemen before the game could be resumed.

And, nearer home, a Mr Craigmile drove into the rough at Wallasey to find his ball embedded in a nest of angry wasps. He was criticized for returning to the tee, but Mr Craigmile considered it the soundest decision he had made in years.

SNAKES IN THE GRASS

Back in the days when Zimbabwe was Rhodesia, the Sinoia Country Club was a favourite watering hole for wealthy businessmen and their wives.

Mrs Bobby Pritchard, playing a round there in 1952, drove for the tee and watched the ball veer off course into a verge of deep scrub. Rhodesian rough held different problems to its English counterpart, but even the experienced Mrs Pritchard was surprised to find her ball nestled in the centre of the coils of an unpleasant-looking python.

The snake remained motionless, presumably waiting for her next move, and Mrs Pritchard wisely consulted the club secretary. The rules catered for every eventuality, and he gave his verdict without hesitation: 'Borrow a gun from the clubhouse, shoot the snake and play your stroke.' If only all golfing problems could be so easily solved.

After taking on the Japanese in World War Two, members of a golf club near Darwin, North Australia, returned to find themselves locked in combat with all manner of other enemies. Crocodiles, snakes and ferocious hawks all lay in wait for unsuspecting golfers.

The problem became so acute that a new rule had to be introduced: 'When a hawk, crocodile, snake or wallaby takes the ball, another shall be dropped.' A move toasted with relief by battle-weary veterans.

MAKING A MOUNTAIN OUT OF AN ANTHILL

The more daunting natural hazards at Ndola golf course in equatorial Africa include six-metre-high anthills, inhabited by aggressive razor-jawed creatures with scant respect for the finer points of the game.

When Australian Jack Newton was playing the seventeenth in a major tournament at Ndola, he was concentrating too much to notice his caddies flee from the green. The reason became apparent when Newton felt his body alive with a searing pain akin to hot needles.

The only answer to such a critical emergency was to do the sensible thing and tear off all his clothes. He hopped around pulling off every item, including his underpants, while his wife dodged around trying to block the view of bemused spectators.

A stalwart woman player on the Schwebo course in Burma in 1939 had to order her caddy to kill a full-grown viper on the fourth green.

The pair following had to destroy a six-foot cobra before they could continue. After this, all players at Schwebo were issued with fire-crackers to discharge before following balls into the undergrowth.

Golf at the Hill Club, Nairobi, in the inter-war years was frequently interrupted by a huge lion.

It first appeared on the fairway between the eleventh and twelfth hole where it seized a caddy and carried him off. The golfer, about to change irons, rushed after the beast to rescue the man, but was unable to catch it.

A few weeks later the beast appeared shortly before breakfast, knocked a caddy flying and trotted off with his golf bag between its teeth.

Finally a visiting English golfer was pounced upon in mid-stroke and carried away to a cave. The lion was shot and the player recovered, presumably to finish his game.

A WILD BIRDIE

As flying tee-shots go, it was not quite enough for an eagle or an albatross, but it did knock a big Canadian goose off course. The anonymous player who stunned the birdie in full flight over the short seventeenth at Silvermere Golf Club near Cobham, Surrey, in 1984, was himself too stunned to continue his round.

An RSPCA inspector waded into a nearby lake to retrieve the bewildered bird. It was released back into the wild after being treated for a broken leg. The golfer never returned.

GOLFER AT BAY

In 1984 the *Sunday Express* carried a photograph of golfer Ralph Parker, a Nottingham company director, brandishing his driver, with the cover still attached, at a huge red stag which had decided to challenge him for supremacy at Wollaton Park Golf Club.

One of Jennie Lee Smith's more memorable moments at the British Women's Open at Gosforth Park happened as she teed off to play the eleventh. As Jennie addressed the ball her concentration was badly shaken by a sudden shriek from beneath her feet, and the discovery that she had accidentally stepped on a sleeping rabbit.

After the tournament Jennie relaxed with a cooling drink in the clubhouse – and was stung on the nose by a wasp.

DANGER - GOLFERS AT WORK

CLUB SANDWICH

When Sandwich returned to normal after the 1899 Open, an inexperienced member took to the course the evening after the tournament.

The gales which had dogged the Open had not abated, and his drive at the fourth was plucked by the wind, and propelled in the direction of nearby King's Avenue.

The ball sailed over a fence, hit a delivery boy a sideswipe and knocked him from his bicycle. A charabanc travelling in the opposite direction swerved wildly to avoid him, collided with a stone wall and caught fire.

The member staggered shaken into the clubhouse blaming himself for everything.

'What should I do?' he pleaded to the first person he encountered.

It happened to be the legendary Harry Vardon, who had just won the Open.

'If I were you,' said Harry, 'I'd try positioning your left thumb a little more to the right when you address the ball.'

NEVER GIVE AN OPPONENT
AN EVEN BREAK

Ulster golfers Jimmy Donnelly and Hammy Gillespie ran up a catalogue of disasters in the late 1970s which Laurel and Hardy would have been hard pressed to emulate.

According to golfing journalist Peter Dobereiner, the day at Hollywood got away to an auspicious start when Mr Donnelly was hit on the head by Mr Gillespie as he bent down to fasten a loose shoelace at the tee.

Mr Gillespie picked up his partner and hoisted him over his shoulder in a fireman's lift for the long trek back to the clubhouse. Somewhere on the journey Mr Gillespie, staggering under his burden, lost his footing and tripped. The concussed Mr Donnelly was thrown to the floor, breaking his ankle on impact.

At the clubhouse an ambulance was quickly organized to get the casualty to hospital. Mr Gillespie, concerned to help his friend further, decided to drive Mr Donnelly's car to the hospital so that he could get home easily when he was discharged.

Unfortunately the ambulance had to brake suddenly in the Belfast traffic and Mr Gillespie, unable to stop in time, collided with the back of it. The crash burst open the door catch, precipitating Mr Gillespie – still on his stretcher – into the road. The car was written off and Mr Donnelly, in addition to his other injuries, sustained a broken collar bone.

IS IT A BIRDIE? – NO, IT'S A PLANE

Golfers never tire of regaling each other about what hot-shots they are. But few could hope to match the achievement of George V. Vine of Newark who almost brought down a passing aircraft.

His disappointingly high drive hit the pilot of a low-flying aeroplane right between the eyes.

The surprised aviator, momentarily stunned, wrestled with the controls but managed to keep his machine on an even keel and flew on.

PUT THAT IN YOUR PIPE

In 1935 a player who had just driven off from the eleventh at Belfriars, Leigh, heard a cry. A hundred and sixty yards away the ball had smashed the pipe of an astonished man strolling on the course, without even chipping a tooth.

Mr N. Bathie, playing the normally tranquil links at Downfield, Dundee, was surprised to see the ball rise into the air as he addressed it.

It was a little breezy at the time, but he thought no more of it until, seconds later, he was picked up and spun round in a freak whirlwind which lifted a wooden shelter sixty feet in the air and smashed it to pieces, flattening his ball.

THE BIG BIRDIE IN THE SKY

Sixty troops aboard an RAF Hercules transport plane presumably did not hear golfer John Gallacher's cry of 'Fore' above the roar of the engines – but there was little doubt that they suffered a direct hit from his 100 mph ground-to-air missile.

It says something for Mr Gallacher's concentration that the lumbering Hercules, banking low on its final approach to the military base next to Machrihanish golf course, failed to put him off his stroke. He swung back his club on the 354-yard par four ninth and opened fire.

Senior Aircraftman Norman Dandy, who was looking out of the aircraft window at the time, saw a small white object bearing towards them. Everyone on board heard the resulting bang and, on landing, the pilot found a dent in the fusilage below the window, embedded with giveaway dimples.

The RAF police telephoned the club, demanding the names and addresses of players who were on the course at the time.

'They said they were starting an official investigation,' said the club secretary Duncan McFarlane. 'I told them to get lost.'

John Gallacher's fellow players would not let him live it down: 'When we are on the course now, and a plane flies overhead, some wag inevitably looks up and yells 'Fore', he said.

KNOCK-OUT SHOT, OLD BOY

In 1949 Mr J. Meldrum drove off from the links at Crail, Fife, and put everything he had into his shot. His efforts were paid back in full. The ball struck a rock, rebounded and laid him out cold at the seventeenth.

DANGER – FLYING NUNS

A community of nuns in Bournemouth had to be given financial assistance to strengthen their defences against golf balls.

Despite six feet of wire mesh on top of an eight-foot-high convent wall, fourteen panes of glass were shattered in their greenhouse.

Nuns were sent scattering for cover by off-course shots from Meyrick Park Golf Course.

'In summer it was so bad that we were afraid to walk in the vegetable garden,' a sister said. Then, summoning all the charity she could muster, she added, 'It's the amateurs who are to blame.'

CLUBBED

Elated after holing-in-one at Alnwick Golf Club, Northumberland, Jim Atkinson could not wait to show his wife Irene exactly how he managed it.

Unfortunately, after watching him demonstrate on their back lawn, Mrs Atkinson was in stitches – ten of them. Her husband, who accidentally clubbed her on the head, explained: 'She stood a bit too close.'

FOR THOSE IN PERIL ON THE TEE

The *Daily Sketch* in 1955 carried the story of a mishap at Ladbrook Park, Warwick, when Mrs Phyllis Thomas had to be dragged out of deep mud after driving the ball near the fourteenth green.

'She walked up to the ball and sank up to her thighs,' the report read. 'She was still sinking when two other women grabbed her wrists and dragged her clear.

'Mrs Thomas, of Robin Hood Golf Club, went on playing in the annual Beeley Bowl Competition.

'But on the eighteenth fairway she fell to her knees in a faint and was carried to the clubhouse.

'Mrs Thomas said: "I only played the rest of the round because of my partner".'

The *Daily Telegraph* in 1932 gave an account, under the breezy heading 'Golf Goes Gay', of what must have been a harrowing game at Thames Ditton and Esher.

George Ashdown, the club pro, teed up the ball on the forehead of Miss Ena Shaw, a North London nurse. She lay on the ground throughout the game with the tee peg fastened to her head with an elastic band.

'The professional,' said the *Telegraph* sanguinely, 'hit some splendid strokes and won comfortably by seven up with five to play.' There was no further reference to Miss Shaw.

NO KIDDING

At the second hole of a 'friendly' match at Falkirk Tryst Golf Course, players watched with apprehension as a ball soared towards a woman attending a pram.

When the child suddenly started crying and she lifted it into her arms, horrified players rushed over fearing the worst.

They discovered that the baby had begun to cry and was plucked from the pram a split-second before the golf ball thudded in.

COURSE BEHAVIOUR

THE BURNING BUSH

Mr F. Morton of Chesington, Surrey, could be forgiven for believing that Moses' spiritual home was on the North Sea links at Carnoustie, in Scotland.

When Mr Morton was playing the sixteenth tee on holiday in 1973, a gorse bush, dried to tinderwood in the drought, spontaneously burst into flames alongside him. Flames quickly spread throughout the bracken, and were fanned by a light breeze into an inferno.

Mr Morton played on with his friends, determined not to be distracted, and hastily adapting the rules whenever the ball disappeared into the roaring, red-hot scrub.

Firemen from Dundee bounced across the course in their tender, alerted by the committee, but Mr Morton played on. He just managed to complete his round before smoke and burning brushwood engulfed the final tee.

GOLF IS WHERE YOU FIND IT

Courses in far-flung parts of the world have gamely adapted to the rigours of local terrain.

'A ball landing in a land-crab's hole may be lifted without penalty,' ran a sensible rule at Port Blair in the Andaman Islands. Assuming, of course, that the crab was not at home at the time.

On a course in Jinja, Uganda, a player could 'remove his ball from the footprint of a hippopotamus without penalty.'

Golf was at one time impossible for six months of the year on the equatorial course at Guayaquil, Ecuador, because the baked-clay fairway lay under floodwater.

Then a golfing engineer solved the problem – by concreting the greens. Visitors playing a high pitch were surprised to see their ball bounce once and disappear forever into the wide blue yonder.

Some rather nippy rounds were played at one course in the Congo which had nine holes, laid out around giant anthills, bigger than houses.

One of the world's toughest courses must be at Port Stanley in the Falklands.

The nine-hole course, complete with booby-trapped bunkers, is in the middle of a former Argentinian minefield.

Scots lance-corporal Chris White wrote to the Royal and Ancient demanding rules covering mines and low-flying aircraft. On the credit side, it was fairly easy to foxhole in one.

HERE'S MUD IN YOUR EYE

Honolulu's Hole-In-One Golf Club has a nine-teenth tee on the edge of an active volcano, but even that could not be as gruelling as golf in Roturua, New Zealand.

The course, in an area of intense underground thermal activity, often has holes blown in the fairway by eruptions. Flushed golfers return to the clubhouse spattered with hot mud.

Hundreds of balls are lost each year in craters of the foul-smelling, bubbling stuff. Only hot-shots, they say, manage to complete the course.

PLAYING BY THE BOOK

In 1948 Rule 2 of the Kisumu Golf Club in equatorial Africa wisely stated: 'If a ball comes to rest in dangerous proximity to a hippopotamus, or a crocodile, another ball may be dropped.'

The Deal correspondent of the *Daily Chronicle* telegraphed a sighting of a strange golf match in the 1920s – six miles out to sea on the Goodwin Sands.

Members of Deal, Walmer and Kingsdown Golf Club sailed out to the bank, which is exposed by the tide for only two hours.

Mr Willie Irvine Hunter, who sank to the ankles, managed a stalwart 230-yard drive, scattering a flock of seagulls.

Play on the fifteen-yard sandbank was difficult because the balls did not float. The game progressed by using the periscope of a sunken German U-boat as a guidepost.

DIGGING IN

The stately progress of the 1976 Classic at Elephant Hills, near Africa's Victoria Falls, was seriously interrupted by bursts of machine-gun fire from local terrorists. Among the club's present rules is provision for a stroke to be played again 'if interrupted by gunfire or sudden explosion.'

THE LEAST POPULAR COURSE

How like a Scot to design a golf course for maximum economy. The Polar Bear Club, on Mount Dundas, Greenland, is so cold that it has only been used once a year since a Scot laid it out sixteen years ago.

A team of dedicated diehards from Greenland air base keep it from falling into disuse by playing an annual round with a red ball for easy visibility.

Golfers tossing restlessly in their sleep after a day of missed opportunities may dream of playing in Peru.

The course at Tuctu – 15,565 ft above sea level

– is perfect for driving. At that height it has to be – the air is so thin that balls travel tremendous distances. Provided, of course, that you can cope with the altitude sickness.

A SHORT DRIVE THROUGH LONDON

In 1919 members of a London club decided to settle a bet by playing a game of golf – through the city.

The aim was to tee-off at Piccadilly and head for the Bank of England without losing the ball, breaking any windows or being arrested.

At dawn on a damp Sunday morning a surprised night-watchman witnessed the first apprehensive drive towards Lower Regent Street. The ball narrowly missed a passing taxi, rolled with the slope of the road and managed to trickle into Waterloo Place in one.

A rebound from a lamp-post cost a shot. But the player, gaining confidence at each street junction, doggedly made it to Trafalgar Square as the ball richochetted off doors and threatened to decapitate unwary pigeons.

There was a brief moment of anxiety when he was badly bunkered in the gents at Charing Cross station. And there was trouble, too, at the Law courts, as a window vibrated dangerously, almost forcing the party to take to its heels, but eventually he reached the Bank and collected his winnings.

The challenge was taken up again in 1930 by Richard Sutton, of White's. He accepted a bet that he could not putt a ball from Tower Bridge to his club in less than 2,000 strokes. The condition was that he had to play through busy streets in daylight.

Gamely he set off and, despite the rigours of rush-hour traffic, won easily in just 142 strokes.

It was, of course, only a matter of time before America took a swipe at the challenge. William Patten, of Alleghany Club, Pittsburgh, attempted to drive a ball through four-and-a-half miles of streets in 150 strokes.

A tall order, but he got round in 119 without being arrested and collected his £800 wager. Then Patten quietly went back and settled an £80 bill for damage to shop windows.

TOWERING RECORD

In 1976 the lure of golf brought the heart of Paris to a standstill. Police closed the Champ de Mars, at the foot of the Eiffel Tower, to enable Arnold Palmer to improve his drive.

The maestro attempted to break his distance

record by driving from the second platform of the tower. His best shot – 402 yards – was marred only by a sideways drift which bent it off course to ricochet off the roof of a bus going about its business on a nearby boulevarde.

CLIMB EVERY MOUNTAIN

EFFINGHAM CHEEK

In the early days of nudism in the 1930s, there were more enthusiasts than clubs to contain them. Some would make for any secluded spot to shed their clothes.

One lone nudist, thinking he had at last found freedom, lay down to sunbathe, unaware that he was in the rough at Effingham Golf Club, Surrey.

He was spotted by two ladies in tweeds about to play onto the eighteenth green. One of them marched up and demanded: 'Are you a member?'

The nudist sat up in some confusion and replied, 'No, ma'am.' Whereupon the lady hit him over the head with her club and floored him.

HEAVY WEATHER

The German Golf Championship at Baden Baden in 1923 was played in three inches of mud.

Every player lost his balls, to say nothing of

his temper. The winner cleverly outflanked everyone by driving his ball into the rough, where the going was easier, at every opportunity.

NO CRACKS PLEASE

A puce and spluttering golfer once threatened to sue Bloemfontein Club when 'one of the best shots of my career, straight down the fairway,' was lost down a gaping crack caused by the drought.

WATERING HOLE

Golfers loitering at the sixteenth on St Augustine's Links, in Kent, were for many years accustomed to an unusual ritual.

Once a year an assortment of church dignitaries knelt by the green to drink muddy water from a nearby stream. It was at the sixteenth, in AD 597, they informed the Committee, that St Augustine refreshed himself. The warden of nearby St Augustine's College and officials re-enacted the scene annually. Play doubtless continued around them.

BACK SEAT DRIVING

Golfers have had to navigate around many strange obstructions in their time. One of the most challenging was a saloon car in the middle of the eighteenth tee at Sydney's Chatswood Club in 1965.

The vehicle had rolled off a nearby road, turned over three times and come to rest, the right way up, between the members' markers.

Players, anxious to observe the rules, faced the possibility of teeing-off from inside the car. Fortunately the club secretary intervened to announce that there would be no need for back seat driving.

Another problem to stretch the rules to the limit confronted two British holidaymakers who had a round at Le Touquet in 1957. Both husband and wife hooked their shots left of the second hole. They came across the balls, nestling in the long grass, exactly one on top of the other.

Get out of that one.

GORSE STREWTH

Golfer Robert Johnson laid a tricky shot at Strathlene, Scotland, in 1937.

At the fourth hole the ball rose high and fell into a clump of gorse. It stuck fast about four feet from the ground, swaying wildly in a strong wind.

Mr Johnson gamely played his prickly problem through with great difficulty.

GREAT GOLFING GEISHAS

The Japanese, who have a healthy passion for golf, are not content to amuse themselves hacking balls down a fairway – they have a desperate need for glamour, too. To accommodate this insatiable urge, Keiichi Kozu launched a 'leisure partner club', where jaded businessmen can hire golfing geishas to play a few holes with them.

True to Japanese tradition, the girls selected are guaranteed not to play better golf than their partners.

'It would be embarrassing for the customer if the girls were too good at sport,' said Kozu diplomatically.

There are two hundred dazzling volunteers, aged between eighteen and twenty-five, on the books – and all of them single. A player registers in the clubhouse – the joining fee is £150 plus £40 annual subscription – and thumbs through an album of photographs. Each is captioned with the girl's name, occupation, golf experience and 'charm score'.

'Club regulations prohibit customers from requesting companionship once the round of golf is over,' said Kozu. 'But, of course, the final decision on dating is up to the women themselves.'

THE ARMCHAIR GOLF PRO

Gerry Austin's first step on the path to becoming a millionaire was to bet the outcome of a golf match with a friend.

Some time later he gave up his job as a company excutive to devote his time to studying golf via video and lay bets on tournaments. Gerry, forty-five, lives in Las Vegas and wagers £2 million a month on big matches. Even on a bad day he reckons he has been ahead by £14.

The only drawback is the regular mail from his mother. She berates him for not earning an 'honest' living, and bombards him with literature on the evils of gambling.

ALL MOD. CONS

The United Kingdom's most remote golf course – in the Outer Skerries, off the Shetlands – was put up for sale for £45,000 in 1984. The nine-hole course, set on the 58-acre isle of Grunay, could be reached only by outboard dinghy or kayak –

both of which were included in the sale. The greenkeepers, also thrown in, were a small flock of sheep.

BIB AND TUCKER

Golf club dinners were no mere annual event years ago. The early days of golf were intensely social, each round being followed by colossal communal meals.

Any player excusing himself from the daunting feast was considered a bounder. In 1785, Captain Fairfax of Musselburgh Golf Club was fined one shilling for 'playing on the links and not dining.'

In 1753 another Musselburgh member, David Lyon, was blackballed for creeping away and 'dining in another house' after a round.

Golfers had to dress correctly too. Each club had its own uniform, to be worn both on and off the green. The Royal and Ancient Club decided to buy new jackets in 1780 – red with yellow buttons – and members were fined a magnum of claret when caught without them.

LAWNMOWER AND MAKE-UP

After three long, hot months without rain, the staff at St Andrew's watched the green turf turn progressively sun-scorched and brown as the 1984 British Open drew nearer.

Links supervisor Walter Woods decided that something had to be done. So, armed with aerosols of green, non-toxic paint his team retouched the grass to its natural shade just in time for the championship.

SOD IT

The magazine *Answers* in 1927 reported a ball which turned out to be something of a sod to play.

After several days of heavy rain, a golfer hit his ball into a grass pot-bunker. The ground was extremely soft and the ball embedded itself deeply in a loaf-size lump of turf.

As no provision appeared to have been made for this in the rules, he had to play the heavy sod on for some time before the ball dislodged itself.

BUNKER TROUBLE

Golfers at Denham, Buckinghamshire, glanced up from the eighteenth fairway in 1985 to discover a light aircraft lining up for an emergency landing. The £20,000 Cheetah plane had developed engine trouble at 200 feet and the golf course was the only available place to bring it down.

Unhappily, a bunker provided the same obstacle for a pilot as is intended for golfers. The aircraft tore off a wing and broke up, leaving the pilot, Peter Steggles, to step out uninjured, followed by his pupil, Mrs Majorie Budden, who suffered a fractured finger. Play was naturally resumed after touchdown.

BE PREPARED

The Earl of Balfour, while playing the old Tooting Bec Course, chipped a shot into the fork of a tree.

The rule then was that the ball must be played from where it was found, or the hole forfeited. His Lordship, prepared for any contingency, astonished his partner by producing a ladder from the clubhouse. The earl climbed to the top, played the ball out and went on to win the hole.

LAND OF THE RISING YEN

There were few clubs more British than the rolling acres of Old Thorns Golf Club, at Liphook in Hampshire. Visitors who have not played the course for some time may be surprised to be greeted by a sign pointing to 'Japanese lockers and clubhouse.'

Since the club was purchased by a Japanese company in 1982, locker rooms have been fitted with sunken baths and facilities for players to soap themselves under low showers. Elsewhere there are matted floors and tables designed to eat from while sitting cross-legged.

Happily, no-one has yet committed hara-kiri after a disastrous game.

ROUGH STUFF

Golfers gather regularly on a course at Banbury, Oxfordshire, to play an awful game. This may come as no surprise to some cynics, but in fact they are members of the Bad Golfers' Society.

All players get a warning not to damage the course as they hack their way round. The worst gets a special trophy.

RIGHT ON THE PIN

In September 1907, Bobbie Andrew, a member of the Royal and Ancient Club, drove a ball which dramatically veered off course and headed for a woman crossing the links.

The shot made headline news by striking the point of her hatpin with such force that it remained firmly impaled in position. The woman was unhurt.

THE LITTLE HOUSE ON THE FAIRWAY

Mr H.F.B. Tubbs hit a bad patch in the 1925 Westward Ho! amateur golf championship.

At the twentieth hole of the match against the Hon. Michael Scott, his shot from the corner of the green went over a ditch and underneath a tool shed.

When the referee decided that the ball could still be played, Mr Tubbs appealed to a group of twenty spectators to give him a hand. Together they lifted the shed from over the ball, moved it several feet to one side, and he played on.

THE GOLFER'S GAG BAG

Ernest Forbes

'Does he think about golf all the time?'
'No, but when he thinks, he thinks about golf.'

A golfer: One who shouts fore, takes seven, and puts down five.

'I play golf every day to keep fit.'
'Fit for what?'
'More golf.'

'Is that my pal in the bunker? . . . Or did the bastard get on to the green?'

THE GOLFER'S GAG BAG
You can drive it like a car, putt it like a shot, slice it like a cake, hook it like a fish – it's still a bloody golf ball!

Futura Publications
Non-Fiction/Humour
0 7088 3021 8

The Futura Library of Comic Speeches

COMIC SPEECHES FOR SPORTSMEN

For all but the most extrovert, speech-making is an occasion to dread. How do you start? What do you say? What do you do if they don't laugh? Is the cracker of a joke you heard down the pub suitable for the local WI?

THE FUTURA LIBRARY OF COMIC SPEECHES is a new series designed to give you the essentials of a successful, funny speech. Here is all you need to structure a talk, advice on delivery and timing, and a wealth of anecdotes, jokes, shaggy dog stories and strange facts, all geared to the particular audience you're addressing – in this case the world of Sport.

Entertain your audience – and enjoy yourself with THE FUTURA LIBRARY OF COMIC SPEECHES.

Futura Publications
Non-Fiction/Humour
0 7088 2985 6

THE BOOK OF HEROIC FAILURES

Stephen Pile

'Are you fed up with all these books telling you how to be a success? Are you dreadful at most things you try? Here at long last is a book in praise of spectacular failure and people who can't do a thing'
Namib Times

'One of the few books to make me laugh out loud'
Sunday Express

'One of the funniest and most entertaining books I have dipped into for a long time'
Country Life

'(A) splendid panorama of non-achievement'
Sunday Telegraph

'As a serious book it's a failure, as a tonic to make your ribs ache, it's a rip-roaring success'
Manchester Evening News

'A disaster'
STEPHEN PILE

Futura Publications
Non-Fiction
0 7088 1908 7